STAFFORE

CW00621100

A CENTURY IN PHOTOGRAPHS

Published jointly by
Staffordshire Federation of Women's Institutes
and Countryside Books

COUNTRYSIDE BOOKS
3 Catherine Road
Newbury, Berkshire

ISBN 1 85306 479 3

FRONT COVER PHOTOGRAPH OF LOXLEY ROAD, KINGSTONE
SUPPLIED BY BETTY JACKSON, UTTOXETER & KINGSTONE WI

BACK COVER PHOTOGRAPH OF MADDOCKS, BURSLEM
SUPPLIED BY J. BALL, KNYPERSLEY WI

PHOTOGRAPH ON PAGE 1 IS OF BETLEY VILLAGE, AUGUST 1902
SUPPLIED BY DOREEN THOMPSON, BETLEY & WRINEHILL WI.

Designed by Graham Whiteman

Produced through MRM Associates Ltd., Reading

Printed by Woolnough Bookbinding Ltd., Irthlingborough

CONTENTS

The Maypole shop, Market Place, Cannock, in the 1900s. (June Pickerill, Hayes Green WI)

FOREWORD

The photographs in this book bring to life the history of this century in Staffordshire. I am delighted that the Staffordshire Federation of Women's Institutes has produced this record in the year that we also celebrate the centenary of the founding of the Women's Institute which took place in Canada.

Staffordshire's WI members between them have an encyclopaedic knowledge of the history of the county, and are well placed to record the events in our villages and towns.

This century has seen the development of photography from the slow, sepia studies using cameras on tripods with glass plates, to the modern coloured 'snapshots' taken with compact cameras. The pictures on these pages not only demonstrate how photography has progressed over the years but more importantly illustrate how much life has also changed.

We trust that this book will be enjoyed by those who know and love Staffordshire and by those not so familiar with this beautiful county of ours.

Anita Murphy
County Chairman

ACKNOWLEDGEMENTS

To all those WI members who so willingly sent in photographs in order that this book could be produced, a sincere thank you.

Appreciation also goes to Miss Anne Fisher who gave her time to help with the text for each chapter and to Countryside Books for the idea and help in making another successful publication for the Staffordshire Federation.

Freda Houldcroft
Project Co-ordinator

INTO THE 20TH CENTURY

(1900 – 1919)

The new century, and a new world, can be said to have been born in 1901 when Victoria, the 'Old Queen', died. Staffordshire was then, as it is today, a county of great rural beauty and intense industrial activity, but the lives of its inhabitants have since changed almost beyond recognition.

The county for much of the century fell in three distinct parts. In the north, bordering the southern edge of the Pennines, were Arnold Bennett's 'Five Towns' – or, as they are more commonly known, the Potteries. This area was shrouded in the soot and grime of hundreds of bottle ovens. The factories were owned by those whose names became world famous – Wedgwood, Spode, Minton, to name but a few. The people of these towns used inherited skills. Generations of one family would work together on their master's pot bank. Probably due to the structure of their work, the people developed their own dialects and folklore. This was still very apparent at the beginning of the 20th century.

To the south was the great spread of the industrial Midlands – the Black Country. And 'black' it was. Vast foundries belched forth smoke, men toiled over hot furnaces – life was hard and grim.

Between these two centres of great industrial endeavour lay rural Staffordshire. From the grey stone walls and moors of the north, the land softened into woodlands and green fields to the south. Here worked our farmers. Most farms were mixed, with dairy herds and arable fields side by side. Cheese and butter making was commonplace. Farmers' wives reared chickens and took their produce to the local markets, travelling by horse and trap to their nearest small town. The carrier's cart was sometimes the only link between rural villages and the market towns. Roads were unmade and often little more than cart tracks, dusty in summer and muddy in winter.

The sight of the very occasional car brought people to their doors to watch, and small boys were prone to chase after them. In 1903 Lord Shrewsbury of Alton Towers began manufacturing cars under the family name of Talbot. Ten years later a Talbot became the first car to cover 100 miles in an hour.

Ordinary people got about by bicycle or on foot, or by horse-drawn conveyances. The horse still reigned supreme on the land, used for all jobs on the farms, and in the streets of the towns. They drew along the barges that carried so much heavy cargo on Staffordshire's canals, when boat families made regular journeys between industrial centres.

Throughout England, the outbreak of war in 1914 brought great changes. Men went away to war and women took over tasks that would never have been considered suitable a few years earlier. German Zeppelins dropped bombs on Walsall and Burton on Trent in 1916, and other towns, causing civilian deaths and the destruction of buildings. There was rationing for much

Jack Holland, son of Thomas and Mary Ann, and Mary Hughes in 1908, off for a bike ride. They lived opposite each other in Botteslow Street and married in 1910. Jack was killed in August 1918, leaving a son and a daughter aged six months he had never seen. (Joyce Moore – Draycott WI)

of the war and families often found it hard to cope – some foods, like sugar and butter, became very scarce. It was at this time that the first Women's Institutes were formed in this county. Cannock Chase was a training ground for Commonwealth servicemen, many of whom died in the influenza epidemic in 1918. At the end of the war peace celebrations were held in every town and village in the county.

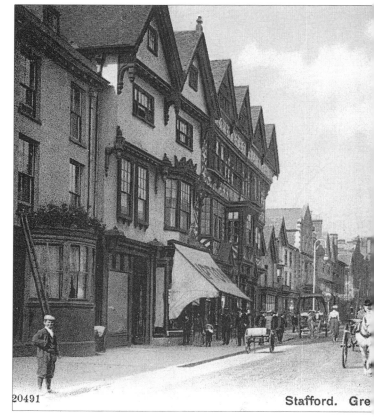

Then & Now. Main Street, Alrewas in the 1900s and as it is today, hardly changed, with little new building. The traffic in the earlier picture consists of two bicycles and a horse and cart.
(Margaret Hopper – Yoxall WI)

Greengate, Stafford in the early 1900s, with old and new street lamps side by side.
(Peggy Burbridge – Doxey WI)

Below The Junction Inn at
Norbury – now much
changed and a well known
canalside pub but then kept
also as a farm by the licensee
Thomas Sands. (Olive
Moulton – Gnosall WI)

Left *Trams running on Station Street, Burton on Trent, c1907. Part of Station Street is now pedestrianised, and although the old buildings remain the modernised shop fronts have changed the look of the street.* (Margaret Hopper – Yoxall WI)

Edwin Hughes and his family at the Derrington Crossing in 1902. (Derek Smith – via Ranton & Ellenhall WI)

The canal basin near East Cannock Road, Hednesford in 1915. This was the Cannock extension of the Wyrley & Essington Canal. In the top right-hand corner can be seen the Boatmen's Mission. The canal was filled in during the 1970s.
(June Pickerill – Hayes Green WI)

ednesford.

Rhodes' Series.

Coppice Colliery at Heath Hayes, Cannock, was sunk in 1867 and closed in 1964. It was owned by Mr R. W. Hanbury and on his death in 1903 control passed to his wife, Mrs Bowring Hanbury. She took a particular interest in the welfare of the miners, and the pit became known locally as 'The Fair Lady'. (June Pickerill – Hayes Green WI)

Part of the village of Draycott-le-Moors at the turn of the century – bringing the cows in for milking. Today the post office, pictured here, is little altered structurally and is busy serving a wide surrounding area.
(Eve Robinson – Draycott WI)

A view down over Gnosall village at the turn of the century.
(Peggy Burbridge – Doxey WI)

Workmen outside the Dog and Doublet inn at Sandon. Everything has stopped for the photographer, one man with a saw in his hand; the family have come out of the inn to watch; and the barrels stand waiting to be moved from the horse-drawn dray.
(Peggy Burbridge – Doxey WI)

DOG AND DOUBLET, SANDON.

Mary Ann and Thomas Holland, and a rare view of a back garden in 1908, at Botteslow Street, Hanley. He was a boilerman at a local pot bank. They had three sons and six daughters; during the last year of the war they lost two sons, and a daughter in the influenza epidemic.
(Joyce Moore – Draycott WI)

Taking the cart across the stream to the men hay-raking in the fields at Pershall. The scent of new-mown hay was a part of summer. Horses were still the power on the land. (Nancy Whilton – Offley Hay WI)

Cutting and stooking the harvest c1904. Men, women and children came out into the fields to help, though one boy seems to have had enough of working and is taking a break!
(Peggy Burbridge – Doxey WI)

HIS MAJESTY THE KING AND GRAND DUKE MICHAEL AT WHITMORE.

Edward VII and Grand Duke Michael at Whitmore. In 1901 the Grand Duke took a ten-year lease on Keele Hall and he and his family were often seen driving their carriage through the villages. The Duke's most distinguished guest, Edward VII, came for a long weekend in July 1901, when he arrived by train at Whitmore station.
(Joan Talbot – Maer & District WI)

Barton under Needwood decorated to welcome Edward VII. The shop on the left in the picture is now a florist/fruiterer's, and that on the right is a private house.
(Margaret Hopper – Yoxall WI)

19

Below An early motor accident at Great Haywood. It had obviously excited great interest in the area, as cars were then a rarity on the roads – most people who came to look probably went home thinking that horses were much safer!
(Peggy Burbridge – Doxey WI)

Motor Fatality, Great Haywood.   A. & R. Stafford.

*Then & Now – Cannock
town centre in May 1910,
as crowds waited for the
proclamation of George V's
accession, and (below) the
town centre today.*
(Edna Wassell –
Cannock WI)

INTO THE 20TH CENTURY (1900–1919)

*An early motor car draws
the attention at Yoxall and
District Dairy Company's
factory opening day in
April 1906.
(Doreen Showell –
Yoxall WI)*

*Right Frederick Sillito, aged
four years, at Yew Tree
Farm, Wootton, Eccleshall
in 1902. The picture was
sent as a Christmas greeting
by the family.
(Audrey Sillito – Offley
Hay WI)*

*Below Seighford School
c1900. Note the studs in
the soles of the boys' boots.
The master at the back has
his eyes raised heavenwards
– perhaps it had been a
struggle to get everyone in
their place and sitting still.
The school today is named
the Cooper Perry School
after the son of its founder.
(Joyce Williams –
Offley Hay WI)*

The daughters of John and
Emily Heath of Cannock.
Prams were made to last,
and pram wheels came in
very handy later for
children's carts! The girls'
father was a local
policeman. (Grace Priddey
– Aston by Stone WI)

24

INTO THE 20TH CENTURY (1900–1919)

A school outing from Fenton in the early 1900s. Outings were a great treat, as holidays away from home were rare for most families.
(Helen Reynolds – Hilderstone WI)

The opening of Yoxall Parish Hall on 2 August 1905. Hats are well in evidence and the local band is waiting in the background to strike up when Lady Burton appears. The hall is still in use.
(Doreen Showell – Yoxall WI)

Yoxall Brass Band in 1904. Many communities could boast their own band and there was often great rivalry between local musicians.
(Doreen Showell – Yoxall WI)

Right The Whiston cricket team before 1914. Cricket was a popular summer sport and local matches were reported in the press. Mr Ellerton, the headmaster of the village school, is on the left.
(Mary Wynn – Hanbury & Draycott WI)

Top Right All dressed up for the Burton Regatta c1910. The Regatta was held every year up to the war, on Wednesday afternoons in the summer, when most shops had their half-day closing. Marquees were erected by the local breweries on the water meadows by the river Trent; the rowing clubs were under the patronage of Bass Brewery. They catered for different social groups - the Gentleman in the Burton Rowing Club, the Working Man in the Trent Rowing Club and the Professional Man in the Burton Lender Rowing Club.
(Anne Hazell-Smith – Hopwas WI)

William Bate, off to the war in 1914 as were many young men of the county. William, of Little Heath, Dunston, was one of the lucky ones who survived the war.
(Rhoda King – Offley Hay WI)

Red Cross nurses and wounded servicemen at Stone in May 1919, possibly outside St Joseph's Hall. (Grace Priddey – Aston by Stone WI)

Right Munitions workers at Thomas Bolton & Sons, Froghall during the war, producing copper shell bands.
(Mary Wynn – Hanbury & Draycott WI)

May 26 - 19.   Photo by Dutton, Stone

Left The Rugeley &Brocton transit camps for soldiers on their way to France were built in autumn, 1914. German prisoners of war were also held there, and it was a German who was sent to hoist the flag on Armistice Day in 1918. The hospital closed in 1924, and until the 1950s the site was used to house local people and was known as Brindley Village. (June Pickerill – Hayes Green WI)

Nursing was the choice of many upper class women for the war effort, and 'big houses' were often taken over for hospitals or convalescent units. This picture of Red Cross nurses was taken outside Maer Hall, home of the Harrison family, with Miss Harrison sitting in the centre. (Margaret Oppenheimer – Maer & District WI)

BETWEEN THE WARS

(1920 – 1938)

Men returned from the war hoping for the promised 'Land Fit for Heroes'. They found instead unemployment and a shortage of housing. The years between the wars were hard for many and the sight of ex-soldiers begging in the streets was sadly commonplace in the early 1920s. The 1926 General Strike, and other strikes, left many families with no wage coming in. Soup kitchens were set up, children often stayed off school because of a lack of clothing and shoes, and every last scrap of coal was gleaned from outside the pits. Families could apply for 'Assistance', but it meant a means test and many could not and would not face the humiliation.

Those who had died in the 'war to end all wars' were not forgotten and memorials were raised in every town and village. The two minutes' silence observed on 11th November each year at 11 am had a special significance to those who had lived through the war years.

In rural areas, the great estates of the past were beginning to break up. Life in the villages became less structured with the decline of the power of the squire and the vicar. Farming faced its own depression, and it became difficult to make a living off the land. The Milk Marketing Board began to buy farmers' milk yield and it was sent by milk train to the cities. Poultry farming became popular and mechanisation began to make its mark on the land, but horses were still a more familiar sight than tractors in the fields.

Schools had hardly changed since the end of the last century, though the leaving age went up to 14. All-age schools were still the norm, and most small schools had few facilities. The Attendance Officer kept a stern eye on truants and corporal punishment was the result of misbehaviour in the classroom. The three Rs were rigorously taught, and the drone of children chanting their 'times tables' could be heard from outside.

Women got the vote after the war, though those under 30 had to wait until 1928! Opportunities for girls leaving school were still few, though those in the industrial areas had greater choice than those in the villages, where going into service often seemed the only option.

Most homes, in town and country, had few 'mod cons'. Water would be fetched from the well or pump, or from the stream in very rural areas. Bath night meant getting the tin bath down from the wall and filling it with water, preferably sited in front of a roaring fire.

Food was home-grown and home-cooked, with none of the variety that later generations would take for granted. The blackleaded range held pride of place in many kitchens, though some women still cooked over open fires. The availability of electricity and of gas supplies was gradually making it possible to have cleaner, more controllable power and light, but we were a long way from the consumer society we would eventually become.

1920 – 1938

Many families suffered great hardships during the strikes and depression of the 1920s and 1930s. The note on the back of this photo says simply: 'Outcropping off Tower Hill Road during General Strike. Horton. Oakes, Embury.'
(Daisy Clews – Knypersley WI)

William Bath working in the pot bank slip house at Warilows Pottery in Sutherland Road, Longton c1920. The slip house was where the heavy clay mixing work was done. The slip is the even mixture of clay and water, which is passed through sieves to filter out any impurities, then through a press to remove excess water. The resulting clay is then rolled up, as in the picture, before being taken to the making shops. (Helen Reynolds – Hilderstone WI)

William Bath was one of the original members of the Labour Party in Stoke on Trent. This photo was taken c1920. He was also a member of the Clarion Cycle Club, who were all Labour Party members.
(Helen Reynolds – Hilderstone WI)

Mr C. Brown (of the well known local butchers, W. S. Brown & Sons) and two of his children driving pigs down Broad Street, Hanley in the early 1920s.
(Eileen Chamberlain – Maer & District WI)

The Stubbs family traded
as butchers in Great
Haywood from the 1920s
to the 1970s. The shop,
pictured in the 1930s, was
built into the Manor House
on the main road. Ronald
and Charles Stubbs are at
the rear of the shop where
the slaughterhouse was
situated; Monday was
'killing day'.
(Evelyn Stubbs –
Moreton Outwoods &
Bromstead WI)

*The blacksmith, Frederick
Ward, and waggoner
Albert Boulton at Ranton
forge in 1928. Although
mechanisation was
increasing, there was still
ample work for local
craftsmen like Mr Ward,
who was a registered
shoeing smith.*
(Mildred Hulme –
Derrington WI)

*Eccleshall Boy Scouts in the
1920s.*
(Joyce Williams – Offley
Hay WI)

38

Eccleshall school in the 1920s, the children posing with their books. The teacher on the left has a firm hold on the ear of the unfortunate little boy beside her! The school later closed, and the building was for a time known as the Memorial Hall before it became a private house.
(Joyce Williams – Offley Hay WI)

The Williams' family car. 'It belonged to my godmother and as a child in the 1920s and 1930s I would be taken out in it for the occasional treat.' (Nancy Whilton – Offley Hay WI)

This was High Street, Tunstall on a postcard sent in 1932 – horse-drawn carts and a tram are the only vehicles to be seen. (Daisy Clews – Knypersley WI)

The Market Square at Tunstall in about 1933, and cars begin to line the streets – and two policemen to keep an eye on the scene.
(Daisy Clews – Knypersley WI)

Below *A charabanc outing for Fenton Park Methodist Church Sunday school in the 1920s. Travelling at about 12 mph, charabancs became very popular for group outings; there was a collapsible hood at the back which could be pulled over if it rained.*
(Helen Reynolds – Hilderstone WI)

'My great-uncle and great-aunt Reg and Flo Wilson, owners of Wilson's Radio in Liverpool Road, Stoke on Trent, leaving for their honeymoon in 1924 in a motorbike and sidecar.' Sidecars are rarely seen nowadays, but used to be common on the roads, handy for transporting the whole family!
(Helen Reynolds – Hilderstone WI)

Below *Tom Hitchenor in the 'batch cart' belonging to the mill at Kings Bromley. This was tenanted from Kings Bromley Estate – a three-storeyed building with two pairs of stones run by a water wheel on the river Trent. The mill was worked until 1950.*
(Eleanor Taylor – Farewell & Chorley WI)

Samuel Stephens of Fenton with his pony and trap. Mr Stephens, who came to the Potteries in 1889 and died in 1935, epitomised the interconnection of civic duty, religion and manufacture in the Potteries at the turn of the century: a magistrate, brick manufacturer and 'staunch Methodist'. (Helen Reynolds – Hilderstone WI)

A chapel outing at Wetley Rocks in 1927. They were to be the guests of Mr Nathan Bustan at Rudyard Hall.
(June Sherratt – Wetley Rocks WI)

BETWEEN THE WARS (1920–1938)

Horse-drawn drays were used to transport raw materials from Cheddleton station to Brittains paper mill in the 1920s; John Mellor looked after the horses.
(Evelyn Richards – Cheddleton WI)

Ploughing with horses at Audmore Farm, Gnosall in 1933. Great pride was taken by the men in ploughing a straight furrow.
(Sheila Moulton – Gnosall WI)

Four horses draw the binder at Chorley Place Farm in 1937. (Mary Foster – Farewell & Chorley WI)

Above The Griffin Potato Sorter was invented in 1922 by Mr Albert Griffin of Whitmore. It sold for £4 5s, and helped to ease some of the backbreaking work associated with the potato harvest.

(Joan Talbot – Maer & District WI)

Left Harvest time at Little
Heath near Dunston in the
late 1930s, and a break for
refreshments. Home-made
wine was very popular
between the wars, and
from the smiling faces it
looks as if they were
sampling something a little
stronger than cold tea!
(Rhoda King – Offley
Hay WI)

*William Prince of
Crakemarsh Hall Farm,
carrying the milk in the
1930s.*
(Dorothy Robinson –
Farewell & Chorley WI)

The North Staffs Hunt, passing Quaker Farm,
Shallowford c1932. This road has since been considerably
widened and 'improved'.
(Anne Fisher – Aston by Stone WI)

Parade of working horses at the local agricultural show at Lichfield.
(Eleanor Taylor –
Farewell & Chorley WI)

At the Uttoxeter carnival in the late 1920s, with May Langridge as Britannia. (Dorothy Robinson – Farewell & Chorley WI)

*Ipstone's football team –
the 'Black and Ambers' –
in the early 1920s.
(Mary Wynn – Hanbury
& Draycott WI)*

*Maer & District Women's
Institute members at Maer
Hall in 1929 – one of the
first institutes formed in
1919. The daughters of the
owner of the Hall,
shipowner F. G. Harrison,
were both active in the WI.
(Maer & District WI)*

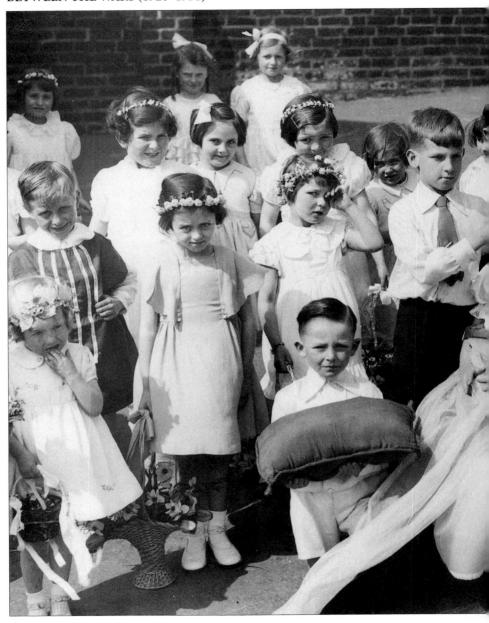

Crowning the May Queen at Florence Infants' School,
Longton, Stoke on Trent in 1938.
(Edna Mullen – Heron Cross WI)

Maypole dancing at Whiston in the early 1920s. The tradition was kept up by many local schools. (Mary Wynn – Hanbury & Draycott WI)

The Rose Queen parade at Biddulph Central Girls' School in 1937. (Knypersley WI)

THE SECOND WORLD WAR

(1939 – 1945)

On the 3rd September 1939 the Prime Minister, Mr Neville Chamberlain, announced to the nation that we were at war with Germany.

The period after the declaration came to be know as the 'phoney war'. The expected air raids did not immediately materialise, and it was not until the evacuation from Dunkirk in June 1940 that the seriousness of the situation was brought home. Invasion became a very real possibility. The wireless, now found in nearly every home, became the link with the outside world and news bulletins were listened to carefully. The wireless also brought information and entertainment, with tips on everything from health to stretching the rations, and regular and well loved programmes like *ITMA* and *Workers' Playtime*.

This war involved the civilian population as never before. The blackout was rigorously imposed. Car headlights had to be partly shielded so that as little light as possible was cast. Street lamps remained unlit, making walking a hazardous business at times. 'Put that light out' became a familiar cry from the local air raid wardens.

Birmingham and the Black Country were extensively bombed, though more rural areas escaped heavy raids. Men too old or too young for the services, or in reserved occupations, joined the Home Guard or the Observer Corps, the ARP or the Fire Service. Women, too, volunteered to do their bit in home defence, fought fires and kept guard at night.

Attack by gas was greatly feared and everyone was issued with a gas mask, even the youngest of children. These had to be carried at all times. Air raid shelters were built or dug in the towns. Anderson shelters were issued for erection in back gardens, and Morrison shelters for indoors, doubling as tables.

The biggest catastrophe in Staffordshire occurred near the village of Hanbury on 27th November 1944. The mine at Fauld was being used to store 4,000 tons of RAF bombs and these exploded without warning, leaving a crater 800 yards long, 300 yards wide and 150 feet deep. It is said that the explosion was heard in London. Seventy people were killed. The crater is still there, though over the years nature has healed the scar with fresh greenery and it is now a place of peace and tranquillity.

Rationing was imposed from the beginning of the war and it is said that our diet then was the healthiest it had ever been! Dig for Victory was a well known slogan, and every spare piece of land was dug up to grow food crops. Food production and preservation were the order of the day and it was at this time that the Women's Institutes acquired their jam making image. With a grant from the Ministry of Food, the National Federation of WIs organised a fruit preservation scheme, and the efforts of the women members were instrumental in keeping at least some food on village tables.

On the farms, the Women's Land Army laboured to keep the nation's food supplies

1939 – 1945

going, many girls from all walks of life volunteering to do this work rather than go into the services.

VE Day in May 1945 was celebrated in style, with street parties, sports and bonfires. Hoarded treats were pooled as everyone rallied round to have a day to remember. Church bells were allowed to ring out again, the lights came on at last and families could look forward to being reunited with their loved ones.

As with every county, the war years left their mark on Staffordshire. The remains of the vast munitions factory at Swynnerton mar a beautiful area and Cannock Chase still shows the outlines of prisoner of war camps. In woods and fields, derelict brick huts mark the site of aerodromes and army camps. Compared to many counties, however, Staffordshire survived comparatively unscathed.

The Home Guard of the parish of Draycott-le-Moors, consisting of members from Draycott, Cresswell and Tormanslow, marching down Cresswell Lane. The unit met in the cricket pavilion at Cresswell and their firing range was sited at Sandhurst.
(Eve Robinson – Draycott WI)

*Edward Trethewey, a
reporter for the* Evening
Sentinel, *listening to a
wartime report on the
radio at the Sentinel office
in Hanley. The radio was
an important part of our
lives during the war,
keeping us entertained and
in touch with events.*
(Susan Clowes – Heron
Cross WI)

*Brittains paper mill had
their own St John
Ambulance Brigade,
formed in 1939 when war
broke out. When qualified,
members took part in air
raid duty at the Moorlands
Hospital, Leek. After the
war, until the 1970s, they
continued to attend local
functions.*
(Evelyn Richards –
Cheddleton WI)

*Wetley Rocks Home Guard
in 1940. They met at the
local smithy in the village.
Mr Colclough was in
charge of the unit.*
(June Sherratt – Wetley
Rocks WI)

Crossplains, Needwood was demolished during the war to make way for an airfield at Rangemoor. The needs of the war effort came first and buildings and farmland were quickly requisitioned and built over.
(Dorothy Robinson – Farewell & Chorley WI)

Girls from Staffordshire found themselves far from home – this group were in the WRAF 'somewhere on the South Coast' in 1943.
(Joy Ball – Knypersley WI)

Horace Pennington being presented to the King and Queen in 1942. Before the war he was the Poor Law Officer for Stoke on Trent, but for the duration he acted as Deputy Local Defence Officer and as such was presented to the royal visitors on their official visit to the city. The job was 'hush-hush' at the time and he rarely spoke about it after the war, or about this photo which was found among his possessions after his death.

(Helen Reynolds – Hilderstone WI)

Corn stooks in the fields at Audmore Farm, Gnosall in 1940. A good harvest was vital as food became more strictly rationed.
(Sheila Moulton – Gnosall WI)

Work had to go on in many essential industries, including here at Maddocks at Burslem. These pictures taken in 1940 show (below) the inside of the sagger house, and (right) the bisque placers inside the round oven.
(Joy Ball – Knypersley WI)

A wartime wedding at Heron Cross. Rationing of food and clothes made it hard to provide all the traditional delights of a wedding day, but friends, neighbours and relatives could be relied on to rally round.
(Margaret Turney – Knypersley WI)

On a lovely sunny Wednesday in June 1944, Mary and Bill were married at Knypersley church. On Thursday they set off for a week's honeymoon. Unfortunately, on the Saturday Bill, who was a captain in the Green Howards, was called back to his regiment. Sadly this was the last time they were to see each other as Bill was later killed in action 'somewhere in France'.
(Hazel Brereton – Knypersley WI)

Right A group of Red Cross nurses and Sandon Women's Institute members during the war, with the 5th Countess of Harrowby on the right. Taken at Sandon Hall, which was used as a convalescent home for soldiers.
(Kathleen Sargent – Sandon WI)

It was over at last! VE Day celebrations in Livingstone Street, Leek, 1945.
(Elaine Pointon – Cheddleton WI)

The memorial to those who lost their lives in the Fauld Explosion on the 27th November 1944. Hanbury was a peaceful village during the war but at eleven minutes past eleven on that November day the peace was shattered by a terrible explosion. Thousands of tons of high explosive bombs, stored in the nearby disused gypsum mines 90 feet below the surface, exploded, killing 70 people and leaving a deep crater. Over the years trees and bushes have seeded themselves in the crater and the area is now again a place of natural beauty. The Italian granite memorial was placed at the edge of the crater in 1990.
(Hanbury & Draycott WI)

THE POST-WAR YEARS

(1946 – 1959)

*T*he end of the war again brought changes to village life. Communities began to break up and small all-age schools were no longer viable. Improved transport also meant that children over eleven were taken to the nearest town for their education. Many small village schools were so ill equipped that the local education authorities found it cheaper to close them and bus all the children into town than to spend money on renovations and improvements. It was a trend that would continue for the next few decades, to the impoverishment of village life.

Mechanisation and changes in farming methods also meant that the small 50 to 100 acre farms were impractical and many were absorbed into larger units. Fewer men were needed to work the land. The farmhouses and cottages were bought up as country residences, often by town dwellers who played no part in the life of the village. This change was felt least in the north of the county, where the more rugged countryside meant that small farms still had to be farmed in traditional ways.

The Women's Institutes were well placed to note these changes, which seemed to alter the very nature of this village-based movement, though membership was increasing. In 1948 a tapestry depicting the work of 'Women in War' came to Staffordshire for members to complete the part allocated to them – it had been delayed from 1947 because of the difficulty in finding the right dyes for the wool.

The late 1940s were a time of austerity and shortages. The bitterly cold winter of 1947 seemed to epitomise life in post-war England. Many villages were cut off for weeks by snow and ice, and some remote areas saw little activity for months. The RAF helped to fly food supplies to outlying places, but such a journey ended in tragedy on 13th February. A Halifax aircraft crashed on Grindon Moor near Leek, killing the six RAF men and two photographers.

The Welfare State became a reality, and the National Health Service began in 1948. No more bills from the doctor, or going 'on the Panel'; now treatment was available to all. Other sweeping changes by the post-war government included the nationalisation of the essential services, including mining. Pay and conditions for miners gradually began to improve.

Owning your own car became a possibility for many people, and increasing traffic was already beginning to cause problems in towns. The first motorway opened in 1959.

One Staffordshire company that became a great post-war success story was that of J. C. Bamford in Rocester. From modest beginnings – selling a farm trailer

H. W. Taylor out in the hay fields at Wharf Farm in 1947. (Eleanor Taylor – Farewell & Chorley WI)

1946 – 1959

at Uttoxeter Market for £45 – they have today a name that is synonymous with mechanical diggers. 'JCB' can now even be found in dictionaries – a truly household word.

Rationing remained in force for several years. Bread came off ration in 1948 but it was not until 1954 that all food rationing ceased – over 14 years after it had been imposed. People were overjoyed to be getting back to normal after so many years of scrimping and saving. The Festival of Britain in 1951 encouraged us to look to the future, and the Coronation of Queen Elizabeth II in 1953 seemed to be the dawning of a new Elizabethan Age. This hugely popular occasion was also the first time that television had brought an event of such importance into our sitting rooms. By the end of the decade nearly two thirds of households would own a set, and family life would never be quite the same again.

At Royal Doulton Pottery in 1958 – the ladies are making kiln furniture, which is used when plates, cups etc are fired, to stop them sticking.
(Susan Clowes – Heron Cross WI)

Leek cattle market in the 1950s. 'As a small child the highlight of the week was to be taken to the cattle market to see all the animals. It had been a market from 1847 and stood more or less in the centre of the town. It was also the site where the annual May Fair was held which, of course, caused great excitement.' On 2nd March 1960 a new cattle market opened on the outskirts of the town and is still there today. The old market is now the Smithfield shopping centre and bus station.
(Elaine Pointon – Cheddleton WI)

Brittains paper mill's fire brigade in the 1950s. The brigade was formed in the early 1920s and entered into competitions with local firms; it became very successful and joined the West Midlands Industry Group with such companies as Cadbury's, Sanky's, and many more. The brigade was disbanded on the closure of the firm in January 1979.
(Elaine Pointon – Cheddleton WI)

Fun in the snow at Wedgwood Pools, Barlaston Park in 1955, after a heavy fall.
(Helen Reynolds – Hilderstone WI)

The bells of St Peter's church, Yoxall, waiting to be rehung in 1952.
(Doreen Showell – Yoxall WI)

Then & Now. Main Street, Barton under Needwood in the late 1950s, showing the main post office (today further up Main Street) and the paper shop. It is a scene little changed today, as the picture taken in 1997 from the other side of the road shows.
(Margaret Hopper – Yoxall WI)

*Boating at Alton Towers in the 1950s. The grounds had
just been reopened to the public again after the war years.*
(Alan Elkes – Uttoxeter)

*Elkes Biscuits', of Uttoxeter, trade stand in the 1950s –
times were changing in the shops and Elkes had to cater for
the new 'self-service stores'. (Alan Elkes – Uttoxeter)*

Herbert William Taylor junior of Wharf Farm, known as 'Young Bill', with milk churns and lorry in 1956.
(Eleanor Taylor – Farewell & Chorley WI)

Below Wharf Farm at Bromley Hayes, Kings Bromley got its name from the 1840s when it was a wharf area for coal and lime loading (the lime pits being on the farmland) on the Trent and Mersey Canal. The land belonged to the Kings Bromley Manor Estate and was first tenanted and then owned by Mr Herbert William Taylor, seen here in the 1940s (left) with Mr Webb, an employee of the owner of the threshing combination 'Black Bess' (Mr Jack Jones of Fradley). Wharf Farm was typical of many small family farms at this time, still using a combination of horsepower and mechanisation.
(Eleanor Taylor – Farewell & Chorley WI)

*Underground at Mossfield Pit, Longton in 1950. Mossfield Colliery was one of 350 pits in the North Staffordshire Coal Field. It opened in 1819 and was know as 'Old Sal'. During its existence there were two serious explosions – one in 1889 when 66 men died and another in 1940 when 11 were killed. The pit closed in 1963 and the site is now an industrial estate.
(Jennie Walker – Oulton WI)*

*Clarice Taylor, daughter of H. W. Taylor, feeding the chickens at the rear of Wharf Farm, with the stables to the right.
(Eleanor Taylor – Farewell & Chorley WI)*

THE POST-WAR YEARS (1946–1959)

The Burton on Trent Men of Mercia Morris Side dancing in Abbots Bromley high street in the 1950s to an attentive audience. (Joy Harris – Abbots Bromley WI)

Winifred and Freda Boston of Court Farm, Whittington, ready for school in 1947. (Eleanor Taylor – Farewell & Chorley WI)

A Coronation party held at Stone in 1953, just one of the thousands of gatherings all over the county to celebrate the accession of Queen Elizabeth II.
(Rhoda King – Offley Hay WI)

THE SIXTIES AND SEVENTIES

(1960 – 1979)

The Swinging Sixties gave us the youth culture – the mini and the Beatles, and all that came with them. The age of majority was lowered from 21 to 18 in 1968 and for the first time the young had money and the opportunity to spend it as they wished. Keele University was Britain's first post-war university, and education opportunities had never been so widely available.

Reconciliation was in the air, and in 1962 the County Council made a gift of land to the German government. A German Military Cemetery was created on Cannock Chase, and over 5,000 German dead interred, many of them brought here from churchyards and cemeteries all over England. Some had been prisoners of war, others servicemen, but it was agreed that this part of Staffordshire should be their last resting place. Every year since then parties of young Germans have visited the cemetery and met local people.

Landed families were finding it increasingly hard to afford the upkeep of their estates as death duties hit hard. In 1960 Shugborough Estate was passed to the National Trust in part payment of huge duties following the death of the then Earl of Lichfield.

The 'Beeching Axe' closed down many railway branch lines in the early 1960s. Lack of transport in rural areas drove more people from the villages, their homes being bought up by people seeking homes for their retirement. Few young families moved into villages, the movement being all the other way, and many of the last surviving village schools were forced into closure at this time.

The great foot and mouth epidemic hit many farms in the county in the 1960s. Movement was restricted for a time in an effort to contain the outbreak, and hundreds of cattle were destroyed.

During the 1960s anything had seemed possible – in 1969 man walked on the moon and Concorde made its maiden flight. Unfortunately, the 1970s brought inflation, strikes and industrial unrest, with a three-day week in force for a time. It was a difficult period for many in the industrial areas of the county.

Supermarkets took their hold on our shopping habits and spelled the end for many a corner shop. Refrigerators, washing machines, electric cookers and home telephones were becoming commonplace, revolutionising the way people lived at home. Decimal currency was introduced in 1971, although some small shops stubbornly refused to give up their pounds, shillings and pence at first.

Greater mobility and the spread of television to most households brought greater sophistication to village life. No longer did people have to look within their own community for entertainment. Car ownership had increased dramatically, causing problems in town and country. It was during this period that the M6 motorway was carved through the county.

In 1974 local government reorganisation led to Staffordshire losing its southernmost section, which became past of the West Midlands. It was a move not wholly welcomed by inhabitants, who felt the loss of identity keenly.

1960 – 1979

In 1978 Barton under Needwood Methodist chapel celebrated 150 years – it was built after local people had heard Wesley preach in Barton.
(Margaret Hopper – Yoxall WI)

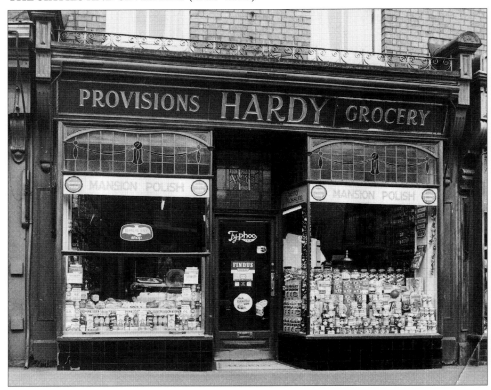

The changing face of shopping – Hardy's grocery and provisions shop in Market Place, Uttoxeter, before and after 1966. Many shopowners had to adjust to the new concept of supermarket shopping and modernised their premises.
(Freda Houldcroft – Uttoxeter WI)

Iris Preston washing her baby daughter Susan in 1963 at their home in Heron Cross – note the open fire and cooking range in the background.
(Susan Clowes – Heron Cross WI)

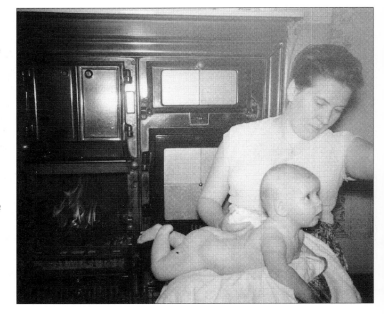

Class Five at Heron Cross Middle School in 1972 – class sizes were normally 30-plus and there were no uniforms. (Susan Clowes – Heron Cross WI)

THE SIXTIES AND SEVENTIES (1960–1979)

The St Lawrence Junior School handbell ringers in St Lawrence's church, Gnosall in 1962. Ringing has been a popular local interest – in 1988 the Gnosall team represented Great Britain at the International Handbell Symposium in Exeter.
(Sheila Moulton – Gnosall WI)

The pupils of Whitmore village school in 1968, the head teacher Miss Dorothy Thornhill on the left. In 1969 the pupils of Whitmore, Nutterton, Chapel Chorlton and Maer schools were moved to a new purpose-built school in Baldwin's Gate.
(Maer & District WI)

A postcard celebrating the beginnings of Joseph Cyril Bamford's firm of JCB in Rocester. Since 1945 the firm has become Europe's premier manufacturer of construction equipment, its famous yellow backhoe loaders and excavators a familiar sight and its name a household word. Rocester also had two mills in the town – one was owned by Courtauld's in the late 1970s and 1980s but is now closed, while the other is now offices for JCB. (JCB Archives)

Above Mrs Jennings, the last to enter the Ladies at Tamworth Town Hall by turnstile, in the early 1960s. After much protest, the council agreed to remove the turnstile and modernise the toilets, with free admittance. (Jean Wilson – Wigginton & Comberford WI)

The service must go on whatever the weather. A mobile library visiting Hopton in 1979. (Rhoda King – Offley Hay WI)

THE SIXTIES AND SEVENTIES (1960–1979)

Right and far right

Lichfield's Greenhill Bower Day, held every Whit Monday (now Spring Bank Holiday Monday), seen here in 1961 and 1970. The traditional fairground stalls can be seen in 1961, with the procession led by the original Lichfield Morris Men. In 1970, the procession is seen in Bird Street, led by the Green Man's Morris and Sword Club.

(Doreen Miller – Little Aston Evening WI)

Elmhurst School fancy dress competition for the Queen's Silver Jubilee celebrations in 1977.

(Dorothy Robinson – Farewell & Chorley WI)

Below Looking down the M6 near Whitgreave. This section from Junction 14 to 15 was opened in 1963 and was an important link in the completion of the motorway through the county. There are today plans to widen it as it now carries far more traffic than it was designed for. (Rhoda King – Offley Hay WI)

MODERN TIMES

(1900 – 1919)

Though change has been gradual, a visitor from the past would find many Staffordshire villages unrecognisable today. A few have escaped the developers' plans and the new roads, but many lack any true centre. Open fields have been covered by estates of houses, old chapels and schools converted into dwellings for commuters.

Yet there are many places of tranquillity still to be found in rural Staffordshire, including wild open countryside now protected for all our futures. Conservation has become an important local issue. In the south there are many rural areas close to the sprawling conurbation of the West Midlands. Motorways have brought town and country closer together, and Inter-City trains reach out to all parts of the country. We live at a faster pace than ever before. Concerns about pollution, noise and congestion affect us all, and as we come to the end of the century there has been no convincing answer put forward as an alternative to the building of yet more roads.

Farm life has changed too, though agriculture is still one of the largest businesses in the county. Farmers have had to look for new ways to survive if they are not to be left with their only option being to sell up to a larger landowner who can afford the huge machines that now work the land. 'Pick Your Own' fruit and vegetable businesses have become popular, while other farmers let out renovated farm buildings as holiday lets or for small business centres.

Staffordshire still relies on its tradition-al industries – like the brewers of Burton on Trent, which has become internationally known as the capital of British brewing. Today only three breweries exist in the town, where once there were over 40 – another sign of the times as firms are swallowed up by ever larger concerns.

Leisure has become a huge industry in its own right. Alton Towers, formerly the estate of Lord Shrewsbury, has developed into a hugely successful tourist attraction, opening its own hotel in 1996 as well as continually updating bigger and better fairground rides. Canals have received a new lease of life and now people relax and enjoy themselves along those once busy industrial waterways.

There are always reminders of the past to enjoy as centenaries come and go. In 1993 the bicentenary of Royal Doulton was celebrated at Burslem. Nine years previously the firm had supplied the first china to go into space, on the inaugural flight of the American space shuttle Discovery. In 1995 the cathedral city of Lichfield celebrated its 800th anniversary.

Computers have revolutionised our work and home lives. Children now use computers in school where their great grandparents would have used a slate and chalk. The world becomes an ever smaller place as communications bring us closer together. Despite this, organisations like the Women's Institutes have remained at the heart of village life, and those that look carefully, in this and in the next century, will find many areas of Staffordshire unspoilt by time.

After 1980

The Mayor of Stafford
measuring the
sunflowers grown by
children at Oak Tree
Farm, Hilderstone on
Open Day, 1990. The
farm was opened by
Viscount Sandon in 1988
to provide training
for young people with
learning disabilities.
(Kathleen Sargent –
Sandon WI)

After torrential rain over a period of 48 hours, when five inches of rain fell in the Trent valley, flooding at Yoxall reached its height on Sunday, 23rd August 1987. Houses, inns and shops were badly hit, but enterprising villagers found a way of negotiating the main A515 road through the centre of the village.

(Marnie Francis & Doreen Showell – Yoxall WI)

*In August 1988 Stafford Street, Stone was completely
flooded. The best vehicle for getting about was the Agrocat,
the County Fire & Rescue Service's amphibious vehicle,
which had the area to itself for a while.*
(Kathleen Sargent – Sandon WI)

High Street, Eccleshall. (Middle View.)

Then & Now. Eccleshall High Street today and early in the century, remarkably little changed. (Rhoda King – Offley Hay WI)

*Then & Now. Hednesford
at the turn of the century,
looking up the town
towards the railway bridge,
with today's A460 running
across. And the same view
in 1992, now altered with
no entry for cars ahead.
(June Pickerill – Hayes
Green WI)*

Barlaston cooling towers, each 250 ft high and 130 ft wide, seen in the distance at 11.55 am on 7th September 1991. Fifteen minutes later they were gone, part of the rationalisation programme by owners National Power.
(Kathleen Sargent – Sandon WI)

The lodge at the entrance to the water mill c1947; and the remains of the water mill and mill pond beneath Blithfield Reservoir, visible during the 1995 drought. The reservoir was officially opened by Her Majesty Queen Elizabeth the Queen Mother on 27th October 1953.
(Anne Webb – Blithfield WI)

Top left *Leahall Colliery and Power Station, Rugeley were closed in 1991 after 25 years, the buildings demolished the following year. This marked the demise of the local coal industry.* (Pauline Chapman – Gentleshaw WI)

A view over the countryside as it was before the building of the Uttoxeter by-pass in 1996, and the new road today. The United Dairies chimney in the earlier picture was a local landmark, now demolished. (Cynthia Nicklin – Uttoxeter WI)

Market Place, Lichfield

Bottom left & right Then
& Now. Lichfield's Market
Place has altered very little
since the beginning of the
century, thanks to the
vigilance of the local
community.
(Margaret Hopper –
Yoxall WI)

MODERN TIMES (AFTER 1980)

Her Majesty the Queen on her way to Shugborough in 1980, pictured outside Stafford library.
(Rhoda King – Offley Hay WI)

Horn dancing at Abbots Bromley in 1990, an ancient ritual which has survived over the centuries. On Wakes Monday the horns are collected from the church at 8 am, and the dancers – a Fool, a Hobby-horse, a Bowman, Maid Marian and six Deer-men – perform at several locations around the village. In the evenings the horns are returned to the church.
(Joan Thompson – Aston by Stone WI)

Above *Wetley Avenue, Werrington, like many other places, was the scene of a street party on 29th July 1981, to celebrate the wedding of Prince Charles and Lady Diana Spencer.*
(Cynthia Hawkins – Wetley Rocks WI)